CREATURE OF THE COSMOS

Poetry Collection

Aurora Aukai

For all who look to the stars...

AUTHOR'S NOTE

Dear Reader,

Thank you for being here.

When life feels overwhelming, I like to consider a cosmic perspective. To be humbled, feel infinitesimally small, and to recognize the preciousness of living beings, and our blue marble.

I hope you always remember, dear friend, that you are made of stardust—a creature of the cosmos. So, go forth, dance, shine through the darkness, and live brilliantly.

With love,
Aurora

CONTENTS

TWILIGHT

Blue Pearl

Floating in the infinite,
in a vast cosmic ocean,
is a speck of dust.

There we find
a grand oasis,
suspended
in a sunbeam,
our blue pearl.

Fate

4 billion years of evolution,
and here we are,
a collection of miracles,
like souls lost at sea.

Spinning in circles

When I was little,
I was afraid
of the dark,

until you put
my feet on yours,
and we twirled,

you opened
the curtains,

to show me
the stars,

and how
they spun

just
like
us.

Looking out

A speck of stardust,
on a pale blue dot,
what better to peer,
into the grand ole' night.

Creature of the Cosmos

A creature of the cosmos,
belonging to our pearl,
a blue and white spinning top.

Marvelous and twinkling,
illuminating the chase,
nestling into the infinite.

We gaze up and wonder,
where is our place,
but we forget,
      we,
         too,
            are made of stars.

Racing

Fleeting fire races,
scripted swirling spectacle,
unrelenting hope.

Another Perspective

For when we look at ourselves
from the perspective of the cosmic void,
we are but a lonely speck
in the great enveloping,
and all our earthly boundaries disappear.

Stardust

Compelling yet finite,
there you are,
a perfect collision of stars
who left you their light,

for there must be
a thousand galaxies
woven in your veins and
exploding in every inch of you.

Masterpiece

What if I told you
that you are a masterpiece
sculpted from pieces
from all the stars in the sky?

Cast in periwinkle
and stitched with ripples of light,
a palette of dreamy watercolors,
dancing in blurred tones.

Rage

She was a storm,

    the kind you chase.

Together

Let us dance in the moonlight,
swim into the infinite,
and escape our Earthly frets.

For it is time to try,
hand in hand,
we will jump on three.

Defying Gravity

But gravity is,
no gentle giant,

so
   sends
        me
           crashing.

Inevitable

What
shall
rise,

shall
return.

Cosmic Ballet

Make the room dark,
and peer,
at distant cosmic events.

A pirouetting dancer,
choreographed by the forces of gravity,
across the canvas of the cosmos.

DUSK

Long Distance

When you are there,
and I am here,
I drink deeply
of moonlight magic,

and imagine a silver string,
a beam of light,
tying us together,
under the same moon.

Gravity

Broken wings,
too heavy.

Paper planes,
angel wings,
anything,
to taste flight.

Up, up, and away,
beyond your invisible touch,
she is always searching,
to escape your gravity.

In over my head

Ebbing and flowing,
kicking and screaming
a suffocating emptiness.

A new day will dawn,
but tonight,
I am drowning.

Afloat

I wish I could keep you afloat,
even when you do not want to be,
and help lift the weight of the world
from your shoulders.

Grounded

But your feet
are still tied
to the ground,

so it will be okay,

for tomorrow,
you will rise.

Survival mode

And now,
for I must leave you,

for if I do not,
I will leave myself.

Survivor

In life's ever-changing tide,
sometimes,
it is enough,
just to survive.

Pluto

We may have dark nights,
love is not always kind,
sometimes for no other reason,
it takes a starry-eyed darling creature,
and sends them packing like Pluto.

Intersection

Let us trust the future to tomorrow,
ride our own orbits,
with reckless abandon,
and perhaps,
one day,
if we are lucky,
our paths will cross,
just once more.

You deserve better

And you deserve someone,
who will map out the galaxies,
and cross the universe for you.

Perhaps

Reach for the stars
they said,
but
what if,

I like the
darkness?

Darkness

Without the darkness,
between the stars
the sky would be blinding.

Stardust

When night creeps closer,
I close my eyes,
and remember who I am.

For all that
I ever have been,
am,
and will be,
is a symphony of stardust.

Bringing me to my knees,
shimmering softly,
unapologetically ubiquitous,
somehow still.

And for this moment,
in cosmic history,
I am born from stars,
and I plan to shimmer brilliantly.

Memories

My heart breaks in the wind,
I miss the idea of you,

but you,
you changed,

and so,
I changed.

And now,
we just are strangers,
full of stories to be told.

Sail

The world was her anchor,
longing to be free,
to sail the cosmic ocean.

MIDNIGHT

Why

One day,
your feet are
on the earth,

and the next day,
you are part
of the earth.

Keeps Turning

The sun sets,
the moon rises,

and
somehow,

the world keeps
on
turning.

In the darkness

I see your face,

in the space

between stars.

Onward

The drum
beat
of my
existence
throbs on.

Greif

Darkness has come,
shadows of stars,
lead me through the night.

You were here,
you were loved,
but now the world
around you
is
quiet,
and nothing feels
quite real.

Overwhelmed

When life feels like too much,
my thoughts are stars,

that I cannot fathom
into constellations

Float on

And so,
we tread water,

like a ship
without its sails,

floating
towards a
vague destination.

But it is okay,
for in the end,
we are all
doomed
anyway.

Tranquility

Sometimes the
turbulent sea calms,
sunlight peeks
through the suffocating clouds
and for a moment,
we can bask in tranquility.

Hanging on

Sometimes the water is calm,
but then a wave hits,
carves into me,
and all I can do
is hang on
to some
wreckage,
and just
keep my
head
above
water.

Still

How can the
universe
stand
still,
yet
the
whole
world
keep
moving?

Air

I learn to come up for air,
to swim through
the dark waters
and scarred tissue.

Unraveling

I am okay
during the day,

it is at night
I fall apart.

Night

Some nights
the exhaustion
hits and
I drift off
the moment
my head
hits the pillow.

And other nights,
my pillow
is a puddle
of tears.

Lighthouse

A moonbeam finds me,
piercing through the darkness
a beacon in the night.

Inevitable

Night passes,
darkness is inevitable
but each morning
I survive
and the sun
shines on.

DAWN

Darkness between stars

The darkness between stars
is the only reason
we can see the beauty
of each star.

For if we had no darkness,
the conglomeration of stars would blind us,
and there would be no punctuation,
between all that shines.

Craters

Like the moon,
you see my
bright side,
some craters
and shadows,
but I tuck away
my madness,
for I am still learning
to love the dark.

Anxiety

The maddening
topography
of my anxiety,
detours
rough edges
of unseen scars.

Lurking in the shadows,
are my triggers,
ready to send me
plummeting.

Darkness spills,
crippling me,
heavy breaths
and tight chests.

Comets

The world
has gone
mad,
so,
stars
fall
out of the blue
flying the savage skies.

Moonrise

It is okay to be afraid
of the setting sun,
the fading light,
and the looming darkness.

The moon will rise,
life will see its phases,
and you,
too,
will dazzle.

Break down

Perhaps it is time
to let myself unravel
beneath the fabric
of the cosmos.

To take in
the wonderland
that is the stars
stitched into the sky,
and lift the veil
of my insanity.

Breath deep,
recharge,
and recognize that:

I am but a
fragment,
sprung from
celestial
seed.

Cosmic Current

Everything we have ever known,
exists within a cosmic moment,
rendering everything insignificant,
but significant,
nonetheless.

Time not to fret,
but to fend on,
evermore,
into the great night.

Cosmic Perspective

The world is exhausted,
so, rest your weary head on hope,
and listens to the repeated tales,
for it all matters,
yet,
from a cosmic perspective,
our problems are
relatively
microscopic.

Fairytale

The constant pursuit of the end,
makes you miss the story,
for what matters is not
the once upon a time,
but the story itself.

Leafs fall

As the seasons turn,
I oscillate
between
cozy sweaters,
and fresh lemonade.

Lush

The forest will
echo with laughter
through lungs
of ancient trees,
and shine
with emerald moss,
as sunset
turns
to twilight.

Nature's masterpiece

Every hour a different hue,
flaming flowers underneath
swirls of pink and orange,
fading to blue and purple,
then a dazzling indigo
with luminous stars,
and a gloomy village.

Earl Grey

Daylight soaks my mug
as I reminisce,
and reflect,
on why I live my days.

The pitter-patter of raindrops,
with a musky novel,
laughter lines
and fallen petals.

The fragile
drunken madness
of 2 am bars closing,
and pizza nights.

Some more

To wander about,
our orb of oxygen,
sleep under a canopy of stars,

and munch on crusty crackers
with toasty marshmallows
and chocolate drizzles.

Tango

Let us break all the strings,
be a puppet no more,
and tango with uncertainty,

spin in circles,
and dance artlessly
to endless beats,

adrift,

in a system of a dying sun,
with nowhere to go,

we can orchestrate chaos,
and marvel,

at how fate loves the fearless.

Fate

Our worlds collided
and now you
connect my freckles
like constellations.

Radiating

And we are
conspirators in pajamas,
toes tangled,
dancing in the moonlight,

with a glass of wine,
drunk with the great starry void,
of the intimate abyss.

Lovely

For she is bound by stardust,
and woven
like a constellation,

with little pieces
from all the
building blocks
of everything in the universe.

Why

Sometimes the happiest people,
have eyes that carry storms,
and salty wounds
that rage like the sea.

Perseverance

We must let our demons dance,
walk through the fire,
let them char our edges
and make us mighty.

Rooted

Would you storm the world?

Or would you pretend
it is easier to fly away
to a galaxy far,
far
away.

Voyager

Venturing
into the
grand ole
darkness,
inching
ever further,
into the
unknown.

Time traveling

As we gaze up at the night sky,
we see billions of miles into the stars,
looking back millions of years.
And so, we ponder:

Who are we?

      Where do we come from?

         What else is out there?

            And, where are we going?

Or, why we even exist?

Our story

Just as flowers bloom
only to one day wilt,

and stars shine brightly
to eventually burn out,

let us dance to the beat,
even though our song
will one day become
once upon a time.

Sunrises yet to dawn

I wish I could put flowers on your doorstep,
and bottle up the ocean,
to bring you:

swimming in the sea while it rains,
the smell of dusty sunlight,
and the touch of hugs that make you
feel like you are combusting.

But all I can give you are these words,
thus, I will press these moments like flowers,
and meet you under the darkness,
so, from our different corners of the world,
we can watch the falling stars dance,
together.

ABOUT THE AUTHOR

Aurora Aukai

Aurora Aukai grew up devouring words and chasing stars in the Pacific Northwest. She now spends her days building spacecraft, and her nights dreaming about the worlds beyond ours. On the days in between, you can find her traversing the trails of the Cascades or traveling.

Connect with her on Instagram: @AuroraAukai.

Sign up for Aurora's mailing list for news about her next book: https://forms.gle/SDVkUYSmfEyX2CQ56

www.ingramcontent.com/pod-product-compliance
Lightning Source LLC
Chambersburg PA
CBHW060532030426
42337CB00021B/4228